Collage Universe Mashup

Copyright © 2024 by Davey Holbrook.

All rights reserved. No part of this book may be reproduced in any form or by any electronic or mechanical means, including information storage and retrieval systems, without permission in writing from the publisher, except by reviewers, who may quote brief passages in a review.

This publication contains the opinions and ideas of its author. It is intended to provide helpful and informative material on the subjects addressed in the publication. The author and publisher specifically disclaim all responsibility for any liability, loss, or risk, personal or otherwise, which is incurred as a consequence, directly or indirectly, of the use and application of any of the contents of this book.

MILTON & HUGO L.L.C.
4407 Park Ave., Suite 5
Union City, NJ 07087, USA

Website:	www. miltonandhugo.com
Hotline:	1- 888-778-0033
Email:	info@miltonandhugo.com

Ordering Information:
Quantity sales. Special discounts are available on quantity purchases by corporations, associations, and others. For details, contact the publisher at the address above.

Library of Congress Control Number:		2024912331	
ISBN-13:	979-8-89285-161-9	[Paperback Edition]	
	979-8-89285-160-2	[Digital Edition]	

Rev. date: 09/20/2024

Collage UniVerse Mashup

Davey Holbrook

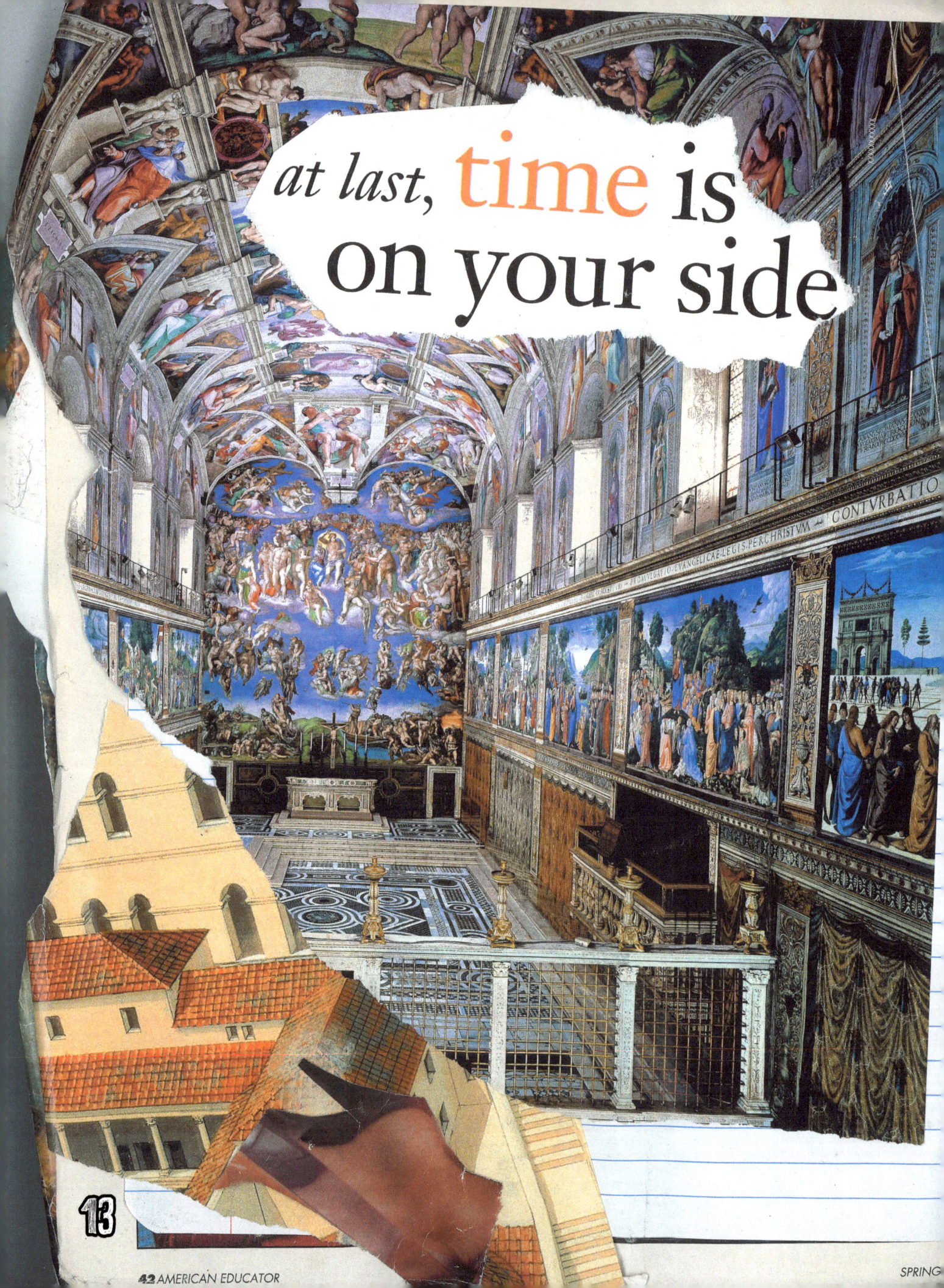

From the BOTTOM OF MY HEART FUCK YOU

THE OFFICIAL U.S. GOVERNMENT BOOKLET

Stop the Whining!

17

SEEING SPOTS

americ

MAY • JUNE 1960

an Youth

heaven's floor. And they sing, melting as they sing, of the mysteries of the number six, six, six, six..."

What I Know For Sure

Is

"The Way You Do Anything Is the Way You Do Everything."

28.

protect

SIERRA MAGAZINE | NOVEMBER/DECEMBER

"...hat humans want. What matters ...wants. What wilderness wants. ...is the only constant."

SIERRA | 3

SNOW JOB

SNOWBOARDING

Attitude at altitude. Instead of sal-chows and lutzes, these guys bone, bonk, alley-oop and pull chicken salad air, Canadian bacon air and something called the crippler. They have as many words for air as the Eskimos have for snow. The new mountain gods, snowboarders, don't wear stretch pants, and never will. The half pipe airs February 1

FREESTY

The Winter Games celebrate man's ability to create risk where none existed. The men's aerial freestyle is a case in point: Strap on skis, pick up speed, then perform a compli-cated maneuver four stories in the air. Stick your landing, or else. The event—a two-jump elimina-tion round and a two-jump fi lifts off February 16.

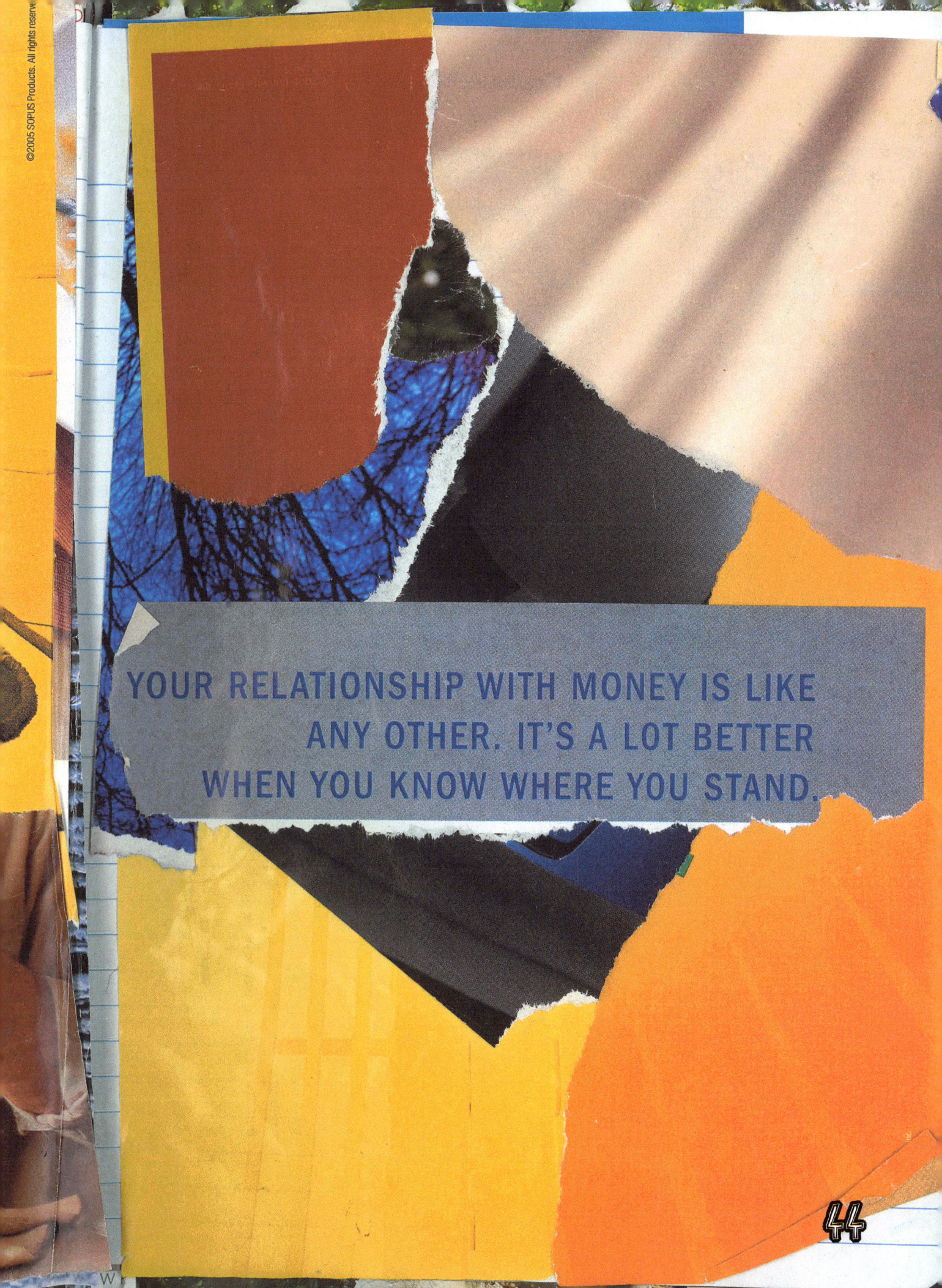

The

...and how

47

mind health

Less Busy, More Burned Out?

Special Free Offer!

RUSH! Guaranteed Low Price! Two Free Gifts!

BUSINESS REPLY MAIL
FIRST-CLASS MAIL PERMIT NO. 47
POSTAGE WILL BE PAID BY ADDRESSEE

PLAYBOY
PO BOX 2002
HARLAN, IA 51593-2217

PLAYBOY

Get it at home and get TWO FREE GIFTS.

☐ **YES**, Please start my 12-issue subscription to PLAYBOY at the Special Low Rate of only $29.97 – a savings of 52% off the cover price – and include all the benefits of the Preferred Subscriber's Advantage*. Also, rush me my **TWO FREE GIFTS**, PLAYBOY's "Secret Pleasures" and "Nude College Girls" collector's pictorials upon payment.

☐ Payment enclosed   ☐ Bill me later

PLAYBOY'S SUPER DISCOUNT SAVINGS

Address
City

PLAYBOY
INSTANT SAVINGS

It doesn't get any better
Save 52% and get 2 FREE GIFTS!

☑ **YES.** Start my 12-issue subscription to PLAYBOY for only $29.97. Plus, send me **TWO FREE GIFTS**, PLAYBOY's "Secret Pleasures" and "Nude College Girls" Collector's Editions upon payment.

Name _____ (please print)
Address _____ Apt. No. ____
City _____ State ____ Zip ____
E-mail Address* _____

☐ Payment enclosed   ☐ Bill me in 3 easy installments of $9.99 each

*By providing my e-mail address, I am indicating I'd like to receive information about my subscription and other offers from PLAYBOY or selected companies via e-mail.

Annual cover price is $61.88. Rate applies to U.S., U.S. Poss. APO-FPO address only.
©PLAYBOY 2002   JAS1020

Get 2 FREE GIFTS

FREE GIFT #1

SOMETIMES YOU PAY $12 TO HEAR BAD MUSIC.

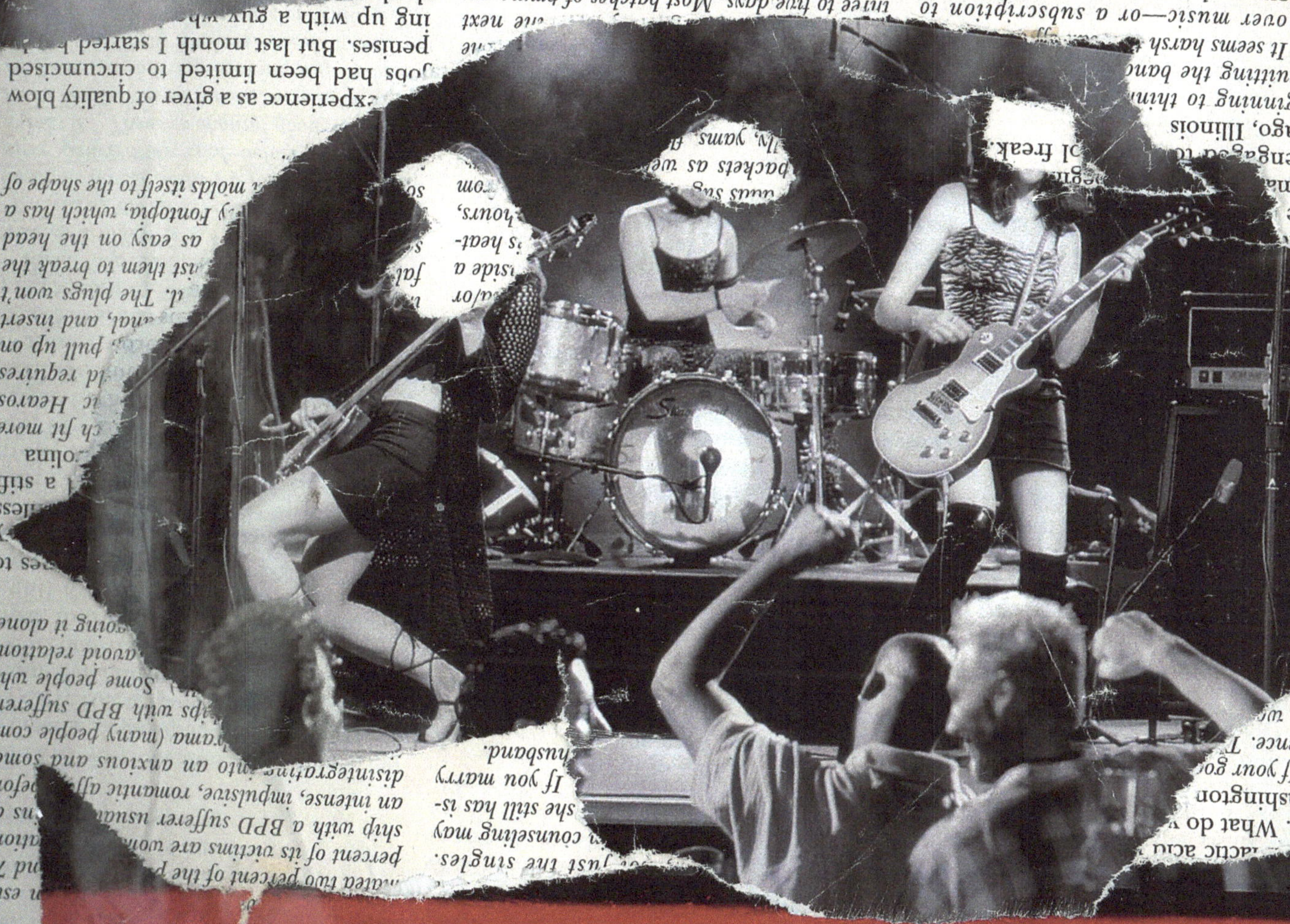

SOMETIMES BAD MUSIC IS WORTH $12.

Questions, Comments, or Returns?
Call us 1.866.386.1590
evo.com

and visit Bryce or Zion on your day off.

Service in the Selway-Bitt
ness, Montana and Id
Work in

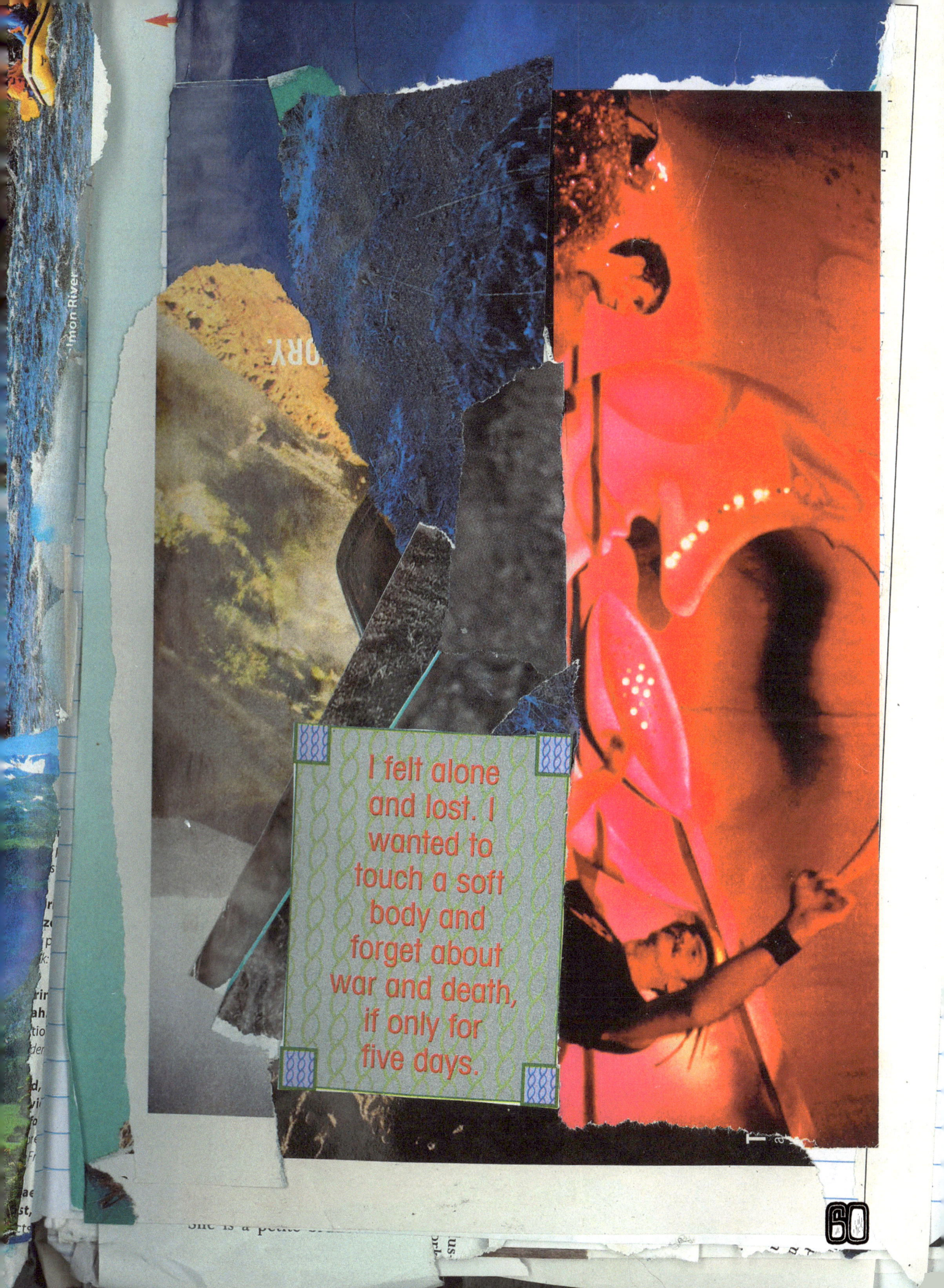

Don't just

FORGET

THE PROMISE

I AM WAY TOO MUCH

I SPENT ALL MY MONEY ON WEED

i miss you i miss you

YOUR NIGHT JUST GOT MORE INTERESTING

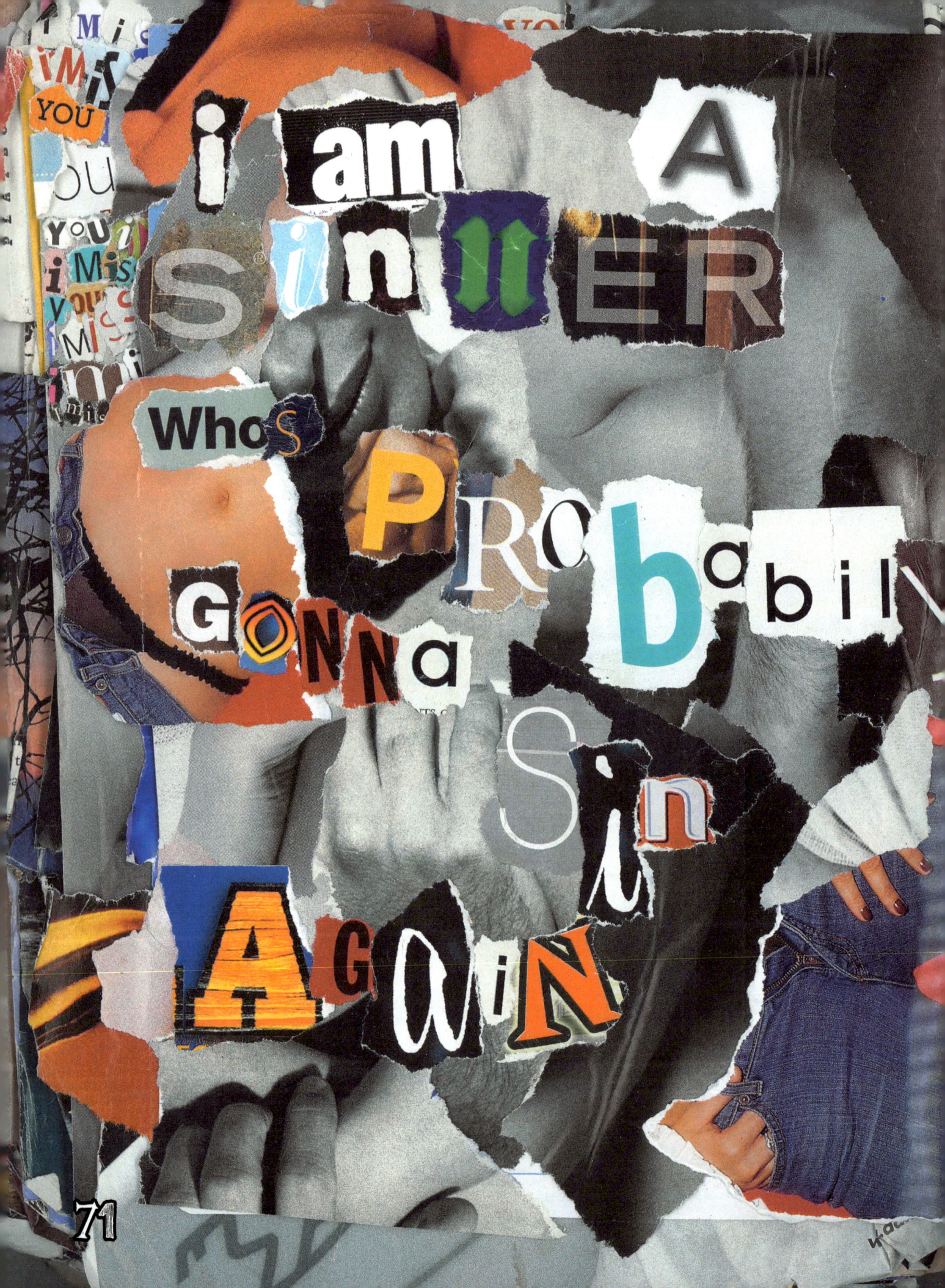

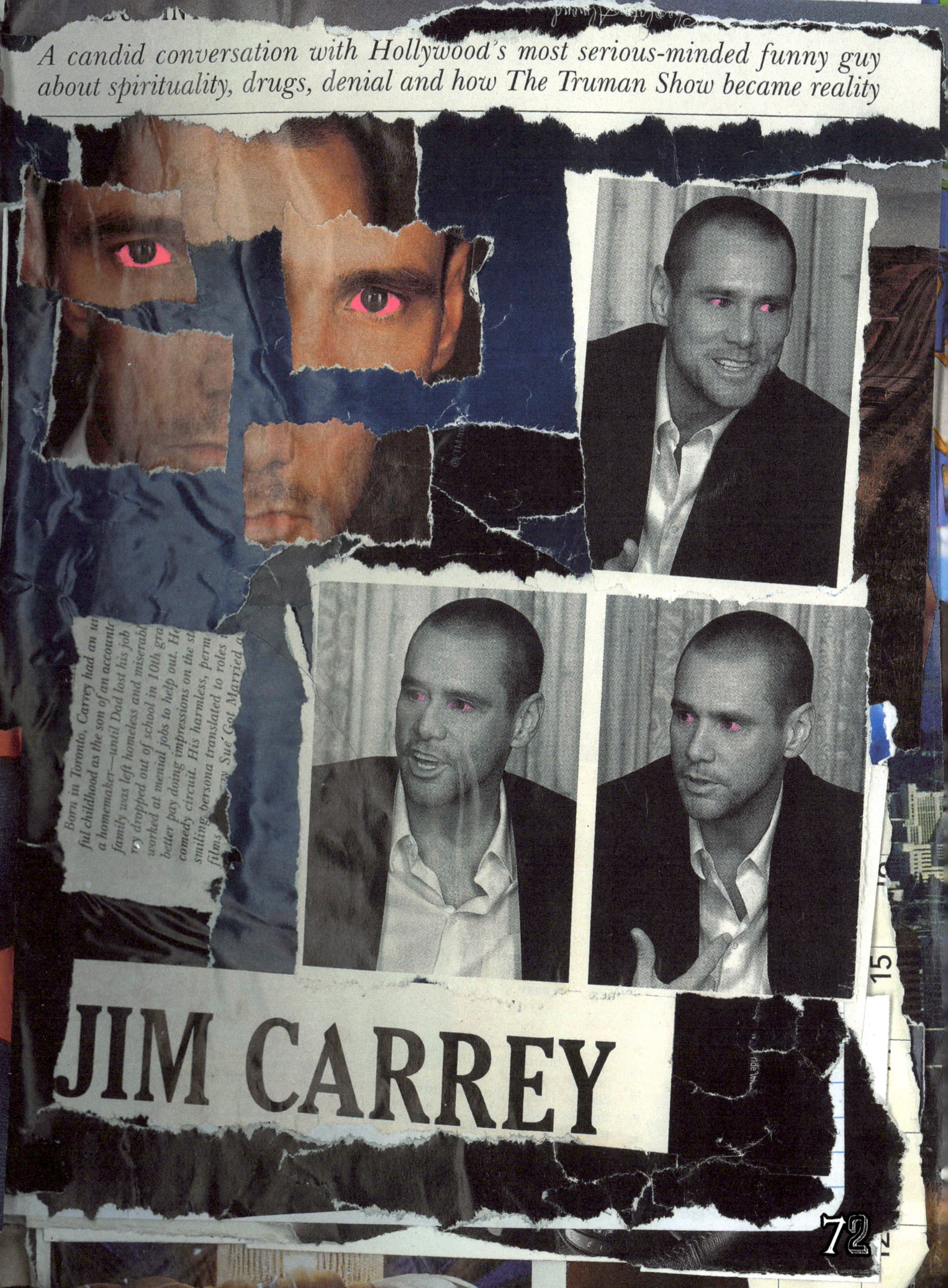

FRIDAY

SATURDAY

SUNDAY

MONDAY

what day is it

when yo
at the
you thi
m

LOOK SKY DO ABOUT

DO YOU Really Know What IS goING on

I can laugh and **be myself** WITH You

THE halF Pictures

ARE NEVER THE SAME AS THE WHOLE PICTURE

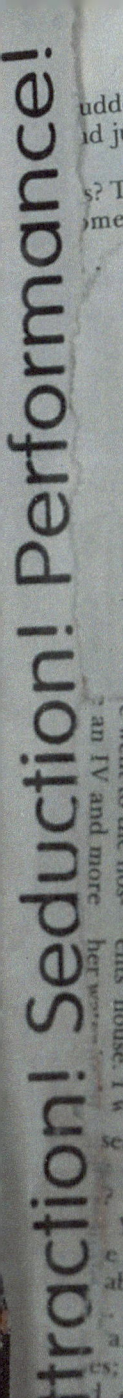

> "I'm only worth millions. Samantha Jones is probably more ruthless than I am."

WHEN I WAS YOUNGER WE THREW OUR SHOES UP

TRY SOMETHING NEW THAT ~~DOESN'T~~ INVOLVE HANDCUFFS.

WAIT 45 MINUTES AFT

"Nothing is good about being famous. You always think, If I'm successful, then I'll have opportunities. You never figure the cost being a total loss of privacy. It's terrifying to have no anonymity. That's incalculable."

"I was never the hippest thing around, which means I wasn't in the position to be replaced by the next hippest thing. I'm more like old shoes."

"I didn't ride a m because I didn't tru I didn't fly planes didn't trust myself. ed my judgment. I t

Playboy Cyber Club

BAD GIRLS MAKE GOOD COMPANY.